SINGLE AND SET APART FOR A SEASON

A Book of Prayers, Declarations, and Scriptural Inspiration for Single Christians

MONIQUE C. BAISDEN

Single and Set Apart for a Season:
A Book of Prayers, Declarations, and Scriptural Inspiration
for Single Christians

Author and Publisher:
Monique C. Baisden
Write to Inspire Publications

For more information or to order additional books, please visit
my web site:
www.moniquecbaisden.com

All scripture quotations are public domain courtesy of
Bible Gateway: www.biblegateway.com

Printed in the United States of America
First Printing

TABLE OF CONTENTS

INTRODUCTION

Single. Merriam-Webster defines the word single as both an adjective and a noun. As an adjective, single means "unmarried," and as a noun, the word refers to "an individual person or thing rather than part of a pair or a group". In addition to us being single, we are Christian singles, which means that we are set apart. Macmillan Dictionary states that to set someone or something apart is to make someone or something different and special.

Since our identities are connected to God as Christians, we need to explore how He sees us from a kingdom-perspective— as this world is our current residence, but not our final home. The Bible warns us to "not conform to the pattern of this world, but to be transformed by the renewing of our minds" (Romans 12:2) so that we don't look like the world or act like the world.

In looking at how God views His children, we see that just like the Macmillan Dictionary, God also sees us as special and set apart. In 1 Peter 2:9, God's children are described as:
- a chosen people
- a royal priesthood
- a holy nation
- God's special possession

So once again, there's nothing regular or average about us. We are truly special! However, as Christian singles who are set apart, we have a great responsibility. We cannot operate and date the way the world dates. We have to be discerning, cautious, and prayerful to know the will of God concerning how, when, and who we are supposed to date. During this season of being set apart, it is very important that we are constantly devoting time to seeking God and seeking God's will and purpose for our lives, in every area of our lives.

Additionally, I encourage all of us to continue to grow into better versions of ourselves, grow with God, and learn more about ourselves and God. In learning about ourselves while we are single and set apart, we learn what we need to work on. We discover what we like, don't like, love, or don't love about dating and relationships. We can learn how to be more Christ-like in our behaviors and actions, and we can learn what it means to be a Godly wife or husband as we are spending time in God's word and learning about Him.

Furthermore, we can use this season to learn or discover our purpose or calling, if we are not aware of this already, and to walk in it. It is essential that we know why God created us, what we were put on this Earth to do, and who God says we are. We are to be whole and complete in every area of our lives, prior to us meeting the spouse that God has for us.

Ecclesiastes 3:1 says that there is a time for everything, and a season for every activity under the heavens. Regardless of how long your single season has been, God has not forgotten about you. If God has put the desire in your heart to be married, it shall come to pass...in due season, in His timing.

I wrote this book to encourage, inspire, and motivate single Christians who are in different stages of their single season. Many of the prayers in this book are my prayers to God. The scriptural-based declarations are my cries from my mouth to God's ears, but also my ways to speak life over myself and my situations, and to encourage myself when I feel despair or discouraged. You can use these declarations during your meditation time on a daily basis to feed your spirit. In the last portion of this book, I have developed a Single and Set Apart Affirmation Statement that you can tweak, if you like, and use to decree and declare what you will work on during this single season and what you are expecting as God transitions you to your married season.

It is my hope and belief that this book will be beneficial to any single Christian who realizes that he or she is set apart and cannot think, say, or act in a manner that is similar to singles who live by the world's standards. Instead, these single Christians are determined to live a life that is pleasing to God in his or her single season. Therefore, it doesn't matter whether you are single and dating, single and date-less, single and celibate, single and constantly tempted to have sex, single and patiently waiting, or single and fed up with being single, this book is for you! I pray that this book will encourage you, give you hope, inspire you, and help you wherever you are in your single season.

May God bless and keep you in every area of your life and in all seasons of your life!

DECLARATIONS

Oxford Dictionary defines a declaration as "a formal or explicit statement or announcement declaration". The Bible states in Proverbs 18:21 that there is "death and life are in the power of the tongue". Knowing this, I developed the following biblically-based declarations to uplift my spirit when I was feeling down, encourage myself when I was feeling discouraged, and speak life over myself when I was feeling disappointed, frustrated, or impatient during various moments of my single life. I had faith that the more I decreed and declared these declarations, my faith would increase, my situations would change, and I would begin to see physical changes in my life, as well as, my thought process and my perspectives about my situations. That is exactly what happened: The more I decreed and declared these declarations, the things that I had previously declared began to manifest in my life. In addition, my thought process and my perspective began to change as I became more optimistic, patient, and hopeful about my future and the things that God had in store for me.

I am sharing these declarations with you, my fellow single Christians, as they have literally changed my life. I have included 31 declarations for each day of the month. These declarations cover multiple topics that a single Christian might deal with in the areas of faith, trust, hope, love, insecurity, God's timing, waiting on God, and everything else in between. You can declare them once a day on a daily basis, or as needed. It is completely up to you. I hope and pray that these declarations will bless, encourage, empower and strengthen you as you walk in your single season.

Declaration 1: "Declaration Of Trust"

I declare that:
I will trust God.
I will not get ahead of God.
I will trust God's timing.
I will trust God when I don't know how things are going to work out.
I will trust God when I don't know when my situation is going to change.
I will put my trust in God and not in man or woman.
I will trust God...period.

Scriptural Inspiration:
"Trust in the Lord with all your heart and lean not on your own understanding."
PROVERBS 3:5 NIV

"It is better to trust in the Lord than to put confidence in man."
PSALM 118:8 NKJV

"O Lord my God, in You I put my trust."
PSALM 7:1 NKJV

"But blessed is the one who trusts in the Lord, whose confidence is in Him. They will be like a tree planted by the water that sends out its roots by the stream. It does not fear when heat comes; its leaves are always green. It has no worries in a year of drought and never fails to bear fruit."
JEREMIAH 17:7-8 NIV

Declaration 2: "I Am"

I declare that:
I am a child of God.
I am blessed by God.
I am anointed by God.
I am highly favored by God.
I am loved by God.

Scriptural Inspiration:

"Praise be to the God and Father of our Lord Jesus Christ, who has blessed us in the heavenly realms with every spiritual blessing in Christ."
Ephesians 1:3 NIV

"So we have come to know and to believe the love that God has for us. God is love, and whoever abides in love abides in God, and God abides in Him."
1 John 4:16 ESV

"Surely Lord, You bless the righteous; You surround them with your favor as with a shield."
Psalm 5:12 NIV

DECLARATION 3: "GOD IS ON MY SIDE"

I declare that:
God is with me.
God protects me.
God provides for me.
God covers me.
God goes before me.
God fights for me.

SCRIPTURAL INSPIRATION:

"Fear not, for I am with you; be not dismayed, for I am your God; I will strengthen you, I will help you, I will uphold you with my righteous right hand."
ISAIAH 41:10 ESV

"Be strong and courageous. Do not be afraid or terrified because of them, for the Lord your God goes with you; He will never leave you nor forsake you."
DEUTERONOMY 31:6 NIV

"God is our refuge and strength, an ever-present help in trouble."
PSALM 46:1 NIV

"What, then, shall we say in response to these things? If God is for us, who can be against us?"
ROMANS 8:31 NIV

"The Lord will fight for you; you need only to be still."
EXODUS 14:14 NIV

DECLARATION 4: "I AM NOT MY MISTAKES, SINS OR FAILURES"

I declare that:
I am not my past mistakes.
I am not my sins.
I am not my failures.
I am loved by God even with all of my flaws, shortcomings, sins, failures, and mistakes.
I am still God's child.

SCRIPTURAL INSPIRATION:

"So now there is no condemnation for those who belong to Christ Jesus. And because you belong to Him, the power of the life-giving Spirit has freed you from the power of sin that leads to death."
ROMANS 8:1-2 NLT

"Forget the former things; do not dwell on the past."
ISAIAH 43:18 NIV

"But I focus on this one thing: Forgetting the past and looking forward to what lies ahead, I press on to reach the end of the race and receive the heavenly prize for which God, through Christ Jesus, is calling us."
PHILIPPIANS 3:13-14 NLT

"But God shows His love for us in that while we were still sinners, Christ died for us."
ROMANS 5:8 ESV

"I, even I, am He who blots out your transgressions, for my own sake, and remembers your sins no more."
ISAIAH 43:25 NIV

DECLARATION 5: "GOD WILL SAVE ME"

I declare that:
God will not let me fail.
God will not let me fall.
God is mighty to save.
God will save me.

SCRIPTURAL INSPIRATION:
"My help comes from the Lord, the Maker of heaven and earth. He will not let your foot slip."
PSALM 121:2-3A NIV

"The Lord directs the steps of the godly. He delights in every detail of their lives. Though they stumble, they will never fall, for the Lord holds them by the hand."
PSALM 37:23-24 NLT

"The Lord your God is in your midst, a mighty One who will save."
ZEPHANIAH 3:17A

"Consequently, He is able to save to the uttermost those who draw near to God through Him, since He always lives to make intercession for them."
HEBREWS 7:25 ESV

DECLARATION 6: "DEUTERONOMY 28: BLESSINGS FOR OBEDIENCE"

I declare that:
I will be obedient to God in every area of my life.
As I walk in obedience to God, He has promised me that:
I will be blessed in the city and in the fields.
I will be blessed when I come and go.
I will be blessed in the land that I possess.
I will be the head and not the tail.
I will be above and not beneath.
I will be the lender and not a borrower.

SCRIPTURAL INSPIRATION:

"If you fully obey the Lord your God and carefully follow all His commands I give you today, the Lord your God will set you high above all the nations on earth. All these blessings will come on you and accompany you if you obey the Lord your God:
You will be blessed in the city and blessed in the country.
The fruit of your womb will be blessed, and the crops of your land and the young of your livestock—the calves of your herds and the lambs of your flocks.
Your basket and your kneading trough will be blessed.
You will be blessed when you come in and blessed when you go out.
The Lord will grant that the enemies who rise up against you will be defeated before you. They will come at you from one direction but flee from you in seven.
The Lord will send a blessing on your barns and on everything you put your hand to. The Lord your God will bless you in the

land He is giving you. The Lord will establish you as His holy people, as He promised you on oath, if you keep the commands of the Lord your God and walk in obedience to Him. Then all the peoples on earth will see that you are called by the name of the Lord, and they will fear you.

The Lord will grant you abundant prosperity—in the fruit of your womb, the young of your livestock and the crops of your ground—in the land He swore to your ancestors to give you. The Lord will open the heavens, the storehouse of His bounty, to send rain on your land in season and to bless all the work of your hands. You will lend to many nations but will borrow from none. The Lord will make you the head, not the tail. If you pay attention to the commands of the Lord your God that I give you this day and carefully follow them, you will always be at the top, never at the bottom. Do not turn aside from any of the commands I give you today, to the right or to the left, following other gods and serving them."

DEUTERONOMY 28: 1-14 NIV

DECLARATION 7: "I WAS CREATED IN GOD'S IMAGE"

I declare that:
I was created in God's image.
God does not make any mistakes, and therefore, there is nothing wrong with me.
God knows everything about me and He created me the way that I am.
The one whom God will send to me will love me for who God has created me to be.

SCRIPTURAL INSPIRATION:

"So God created mankind in His own image, in the image of God He created them."
GENESIS 1:27A NIV

"For you created my inmost being; you knit me together in my mother's womb. I praise you because I am fearfully and wonderfully made; your works are wonderful, I know that full well."
PSALM 139:13-14 NIV

"God has made us what we are. He has created us in Christ Jesus to live lives filled with good works that He has prepared for us to do."
EPHESIANS 2:10 GW

"You are altogether beautiful, my love; there is no flaw in you."
SONG OF SOLOMON 4:7 ESV

DECLARATION 8: "GOD IS PERFECTING ME"

I declare that:
God is perfecting me.
I am growing in spiritual wisdom and discernment.
I hear clearly from God.
I obey God with an obedient and willing spirit.
I am increasing in the knowledge of God's will for my life.

SCRIPTURAL INSPIRATION:

"For I am confident of this very thing, that He who began a good work in you will perfect it until the day of Christ Jesus."
PHILIPPIANS 1:6 NASB

"My sheep hear My voice, and I know them, and they follow Me."
JOHN 10:27 NASB

"Jesus replied, "But even more blessed are all who hear the word of God and put it into practice."
LUKE 11:28 NLT

"If any of you lacks wisdom, you should ask God, who gives generously to all without finding fault, and it will be given to you."
JAMES 1:5 NIV

Declaration 9: "I Am Love"

I declare that:
I am love.
I am patient.
I am kind.
I do not envy.
I do not boast.
I am not proud.
I do not dishonor others.
I am not self-seeking.
I am not easily angered.
I keep no record of wrongs.
I do not delight in evil, but rejoice with the truth.

Scriptural Inspiration:
"Love is patient, love is kind. It does not envy, it does not boast, it is not proud. It does not dishonor others, it is not self–seeking, it is not easily angered, it keeps no record of wrongs. Love does not delight in evil but rejoices with the truth. It always protects, always trusts, always hopes, always perseveres. Love never fails."
1 Corinthians 13:4–8a NIV

DECLARATION 10: "THE WHOLE ARMOR OF GOD"

I declare that:
I am strong in the Lord and in His mighty power.
I stand against the devil's schemes, and I overcome the rulers, authorities, powers of this dark world and spiritual forces of evil.
I stand firm:

- with the belt of truth around my waist
- with the breastplate of righteousness.
- with my feet ready with the gospel of peace
- with a helmet of salvation.
- with the sword of the spirit

I have a shield of faith that blocks the fiery darts and arrows of the enemy.

The devil's schemes and plans are now dismantled and disarmed. They will not prevail in my life as I am now protected by the whole armor of God.

SCRIPTURAL INSPIRATION:

"Finally, be strong in the Lord and in His mighty power. Put on the full armor of God, so that you can take your stand against the devil's schemes. For our struggle is not against flesh and blood, but against the rulers, against the authorities, against the powers of this dark world and against the spiritual forces of evil in the heavenly realms. Therefore, put on the full armor of God, so that when the day of evil comes, you may be able to stand your ground, and after you have done everything, to stand. Stand firm then, with the belt of truth buckled around your waist, with the breastplate of righteousness in place, and with your feet fitted with the readiness that comes from the gospel of peace. In addition to all this, take up the shield of faith, with which you can extinguish all the flaming arrows of

the evil one. Take the helmet of salvation and the sword of the Spirit, which is the word of God. And pray in the Spirit on all occasions with all kinds of prayers and requests. With this in mind, be alert and always keep on praying for all the Lord's people."
EPHESIANS 6:10–18 NIV

DECLARATION 11: "GOD HEARS AND ANSWERS PRAYERS"

I declare that:
God hears my prayers.
God will answer my prayers.
God's promises to me will be fulfilled.

SCRIPTURAL INSPIRATION:

"This is the confidence we have in approaching God: that if we ask anything according to His will, He hears us. And if we know that He hears us—whatever we ask—we know that we have what we asked of Him."
1 JOHN 5:14-15 NIV

"So shall My word be that goes forth from My mouth;
It shall not return to Me void,
But it shall accomplish what I please,
And it shall prosper in the thing for which I sent it."
ISAIAH 55:11 NKJV

DECLARATION 12: "MY GOD-GIVEN DREAMS, VISIONS, AND PLANS"

I declare that:
My God-given dreams, visions, and plans shall come to pass.
It is never too late to accomplish everything that God has
placed in my heart.
My gifts and talents will make room for me and bring me
before great men.

SCRIPTURAL INSPIRATION:
"A person's gift makes room for him, and leads him before
important people."
PROVERBS 18:16 NET

DECLARATION 13: "GOD'S PURPOSE FOR MY LIFE"

I declare that:
God has a preordained purpose for me and for my life.
I WILL FULFILL God's purpose for my life.
I am confident that **I WILL SEE** the goodness of the Lord in the land of the living.

SCRIPTURAL INSPIRATION:

"I remain confident of this: I will see the goodness of the Lord in the land of the living."
PSALM 27:13 NIV

"The Lord will fulfill His purpose for me."
PSALM 138:8ESV

"In Him we were also chosen, having been predestined according to the plan of Him who works out everything in conformity with the purpose of His will."
EPHESIANS 1:11 NIV

DECLARATION 14: "GOD IS MY STRENGTH, REFUGE AND PROTECTOR"

I declare that:
God is my strength and my shield.
God is my protector.
God is my refuge.
God will uphold me.

SCRIPTURAL INSPIRATION:

"The Lord is my strength and my shield; My heart trusted in Him, and I am helped."
PSALM 28:7A NKJV

"The Lord is my rock, my fortress, and my savior; my God is my rock, in whom I find protection. He is my shield, the power that saves me, and my place of safety."
PSALM 18:2 NLT

"He who dwells in the secret place of the Most High shall abide under the shadow of the Almighty. I will say of the Lord, "He is my refuge and my fortress; my God, in Him I will trust."
PSALM 91:1-2 NKJV

"Don't be afraid, for I am with you. Don't be discouraged, for I am your God. I will strengthen you and help you. I will hold you up with my victorious right hand."
ISAIAH 41:10 NLT

DECLARATION 15: "GOD IS FOR ME"

I declare that:

Regardless of what is going on in my life right now, God is for me and not against me.

Greater is He that is within me than He that is within the world.

I can do all things through Christ who strengthens me.

SCRIPTURAL INSPIRATION:

"What then shall we say to these things? If God is for us, who can be against us?"
ROMANS 8:31 NKJV

"But you belong to God, my dear children. You have already won a victory over those people, because the Spirit who lives in you is greater than the spirit who lives in the world."
1 JOHN 4:4 NLT

"I can do all things through Christ who strengthens me."
PHILIPPIANS 4:13 NKJV

DECLARATION 16: "I AM COVERED BY THE BLOOD OF JESUS"

I declare that:
No weapon formed against me shall prosper, and every tongue that rises against me, God will condemn on my behalf.
I am covered by the blood of Jesus, and no evil, hurt, harm, or danger shall come near me, my family, my friends and loved ones, my home, my car, or my workplace.

SCRIPTURAL INSPIRATION:
"No weapon formed against you shall prosper, and every tongue which rises against you in judgment you shall condemn."
ISAIAH 54:17 NKJV

"And they have conquered him by the blood of the Lamb."
REVELATION 12:11A ESV

Declaration 17: "God Is Bigger Than My Circumstances"

I declare that:
God is bigger than my circumstances.
I have peace in the midst of my trials and circumstances.
I shall remain focused on God and not my circumstances because my problems are not bigger than God!
There is nothing too hard or impossible for God to do on my behalf.

SCRIPTURAL INSPIRATION:

"You will keep him in perfect peace, whose mind is stayed on You, because he trusts in You."
ISAIAH 26:3 NKJV

"I am the Lord, the God of all mankind. Is anything too hard for me?"
JEREMIAH 32:27 NIV

"But Jesus looked at them and said to them, "With men this is impossible, but with God all things are possible."
MATTHEW 19:26 NKJV

DECLARATION 18: "THIS IS MY SEASON AND APPOINTED TIME"

I declare that:
This is my season and my appointed time for favor and abundance in every area of my life, and customized blessings with my name on it.
I am open to receiving whatever God has for me.
I thank you God in advance for these blessings!

SCRIPTURAL INSPIRATION:
"I came that they may have life, and have it abundantly."
JOHN 10:10B NASB

"Nevertheless not My will, but Yours, be done."
LUKE 22:42 NKJV

"It is beautiful how God has done everything at the right time."
ECCLESIASTES 3:11 GW

"For He says, "In the time of my favor I heard you, and in the day of salvation I helped you." I tell you, now is the time of God's favor, now is the day of salvation."
2 CORINTHIANS 6:2 NIV

DECLARATION 19: "I AM VICTORIOUS"

I declare that:
I am victorious and more than a conqueror through Jesus.
God is fighting my battles, those that are seen and unseen.
I am not equipped to fight my own battles.
Therefore, I shall be still and let God fight them for me.

SCRIPTURAL INSPIRATION:
"No, despite all these things, overwhelming victory is ours through Christ, who loved us."
ROMANS 8:37 NLT

"The Lord will fight for you; you need only to be still."
EXODUS 14:14 NIV

"Be still, and know that I am God. I will be exalted among the nations, I will be exalted in the earth!"
PSALM 46:10 ESV

DECLARATION 20: "I WAS CREATED ON PURPOSE" "

I declare that:
I am who God says I am.
I am God's chosen one.
I was created on purpose for a purpose.
God has preordained plans for my life that He desires for me to fulfill.
I will walk in and fulfill God's purpose for my life.

SCRIPTURAL INSPIRATION:
"But you are a chosen people, a royal priesthood, a holy nation, God's special possession, that you may declare the praises of Him who called you out of darkness into His wonderful light.
1 PETER 2:9 NIV

"For we are God's masterpiece. He has created us anew in Christ Jesus, so we can do the good things He planned for us long ago."
EPHESIANS 2:10 NLT

DECLARATION 21: "I AM HEALED" "

I declare that:
I am healed in my mind.
I am healed in my body.
I am healed emotionally.
I am healed in my soul.
Jesus was wounded for my transgressions, bruised for my iniquities, the chastisement for my peace was upon Him, and by His stripes I am healed.

SCRIPTURAL INSPIRATION:
"But He was wounded for our transgressions; He was bruised for our iniquities. The chastisement of our peace was upon Him, and with His stripes we are healed."
ISAIAH 53:5 KJV

DECLARATION 22: "I AM DESTINED FOR GREATNESS!"

I declare that:
I am destined for greatness and have seeds of greatness inside of me.
I was **not** created to live a life of mediocrity.
I will walk in my God-given purpose and bring glory to the kingdom of God.
I will live in God's place of abundance and overflow for my life.

SCRIPTURAL INSPIRATION:
"I can do all things through Christ who strengthens me."
PHILIPPIANS 4:13 NKJV

"Greater is He that is in you than he that is in the world."
1 JOHN 4:4B KJV

"Now to Him who is able to do far more abundantly than all that we ask or think, according to the power at work within us, to Him be glory in the church and in Christ Jesus throughout all generations, forever and ever. Amen."
EPHESIANS 3:20-21 ESV

"I tell you the truth, anyone who believes in Me will do the same works I have done, and even greater works, because I am going to be with the Father."
JOHN 14:12 NLT

"And God is able to bless you abundantly, so that in all things at all times, having all that you need, you will abound in every good work."
2 CORINTHIANS 9:8 NIV

DECLARATION 23: "I AM HOPEFUL, DETERMINED, AND PATIENTLY WAITING FOR GOD'S BEST!"

I declare that:
I am hopeful and not hopeless.
I am determined and not desperate.
I am waiting patiently on God with faith and great expectation for God's best for me.

SCRIPTURAL INSPIRATION:

"May the God of hope fill you with all joy and peace in believing, so that by the power of the Holy Spirit you may abound in hope."
ROMANS 15:13 ESV

"Wait on the Lord, be of good courage, and He will strengthen your heart. Wait, I say, on the Lord!"
PSALM 27:14 NKJV

"Commit your way to the Lord, trust also in Him, and He shall bring it to pass...Rest in the Lord, and wait patiently for Him."
PSALM 37:5, 7 NKJV

"Truly my soul silently waits for God... My soul, wait patiently for God alone, for my expectation is from Him."
PSALM 62:1, 5 NKJV

Declaration 24: "I Am Fearless"

I declare that:

God has not given me a spirit of fear, but He has empowered me and equipped me with a spirit of power, love, and a sound mind.

I am not afraid of anyone or anything.

I am not afraid of what my future holds.

I am courageous.

I fear nothing.

I am fearless.

Scriptural Inspiration:

"For God has not given us a spirit of fear, but of power and of love and of a sound mind."
2 Timothy 1:7 NKJV

"The Lord is on my side; I will not fear. What can man do to me? The Lord is for me among those who help me."
Psalm 118:6–7 NKJV

"When a man's ways please the Lord, He makes even his enemies to be at peace with him."
Proverbs 16:7 ESV

DECLARATION 25: "I AM WORTHY AND LOVED BY GOD"

I declare that:
God loves me.
God thinks highly of me.
I can never mess up or sin enough to make Him change His mind about me as God's love is unconditional toward me.
I am worthy of receiving His forgiveness, love, grace, and mercy.
I am worthy of receiving God's blessings He has ordained for me.

SCRIPTURAL INSPIRATION:
"God is love."
1 JOHN 4:8B NIV

"For God loved the world so much that He gave his one and only Son, so that everyone who believes in Him will not perish but have eternal life."
JOHN 3:16 NLT

"But God showed His great love for us by sending Christ to die for us while we were still sinners."
ROMANS 5:8 NLT

"Can anything ever separate us from Christ's love? Does it mean He no longer loves us if we have trouble or calamity, or are persecuted, or hungry, or destitute, or in danger, or threatened with death? (As the Scriptures say, "For your sake we are killed every day; we are being slaughtered like sheep.") No, despite all these things, overwhelming victory is ours through Christ, who loved us.
And I am convinced that nothing can ever separate us from God's love. Neither death nor life, neither angels nor demons,

neither our fears for today nor our worries about tomorrow—not even the powers of hell can separate us from God's love. No power in the sky above or in the earth below—indeed, nothing in all creation will ever be able to separate us from the love of God that is revealed in Christ Jesus our Lord."
ROMANS 8:35-39 NLT

DECLARATION 26: "I LIVE RIGHTEOUSLY FOR GOD"

I declare that:
I live righteously for God.
As I am a part of the righteous and not the unrighteous, God would not withhold any good thing from me.
God desires to bless me.
God will bless me.
God has good plans for my future.

SCRIPTURAL INSPIRATION:
"For I know the plans I have for you," declares the Lord, "plans to prosper you and not to harm you, plans to give you hope and a future."
JEREMIAH 29:11 NIV

"For the Lord God is a sun and shield: The Lord will give grace and glory: no good thing will He withhold from them that walk uprightly."
PSALM 84:11 KJV

"The righteous will inherit the land and dwell in it forever."
PSALM 37:29 NIV

"Blessed are those who hunger and thirst for righteousness, for they will be filled."
MATTHEW 5:6 NIV

DECLARATION 27: "GOD CAN DO WHAT I CANNOT DO"

I declare that:
God can do what I cannot do.
God is not limited by my circumstances and present situations.
God is an all-powerful God who can fix anything!
God is able to do exceedingly and abundantly above all I could ask, think, or imagine!

SCRIPTURAL INSPIRATION:

"For nothing will be impossible with God."
LUKE 1:37 ESV

"Great is our Lord, and abundant in power."
PSALM 147:5A ESV

"Jesus looked at them and said, "With man it is impossible, but not with God. For all things are possible with God."
MARK 10:27 ESV

"Now to Him who is able to do exceedingly abundantly above all that we ask or think, according to the power that works in us, to Him be glory in the church by Christ Jesus to all generations, forever and ever. Amen."
EPHESIANS 3:20-21 NKJV

Declaration 28: "I Am Perfectly Imperfect"

I declare that:

I am perfectly imperfect.

However, God loves me too much to let me stay the way I am. God is refining me, molding me, and making me more like Him in all of my ways.

Even when it's painful and the process is not what I would like it to be, I know that God is not doing this to harm me, but to help me to continuously grow and be a better person.

Scriptural Inspiration:

"Let perseverance finish its work so that you may be mature and complete, not lacking anything."
JAMES 1:4 NIV

"See, I have refined you, though not as silver; I have tested you in the furnace of affliction."
ISAIAH 48:10 NIV

"These trials will show that your faith is genuine. It is being tested as fire tests and purifies gold--though your faith is far more precious than mere gold. So when your faith remains strong through many trials, it will bring you much praise and glory and honor on the day when Jesus Christ is revealed to the whole world."
1 PETER 1:7 NLT

DECLARATION 29: "GOD KNOWS WHAT I NEED"

I declare that:
God knows what I need and who I need in my life.
I trust God's plans for my life.
I trust God to bless me with what I need.
I trust God to bring who I need into my life in His perfect timing.

SCRIPTURAL INSPIRATION:

"To everything there is a season, a time for every purpose under heaven."
ECCLESIASTES 3:1 NKJV

"Write the vision and make it plain on tablets, that he may run who reads it. For the vision is yet for an appointed time; but at the end it will speak, and it will not lie. Though it tarries, wait for it; because it will surely come, it will not tarry."
HABAKKUK 2:2-3 NKJV

"For I know the plans I have for you," says the Lord. "They are plans for good and not for disaster, to give you a future and a hope."
JEREMIAH 29:11 NLT

"For My thoughts are not your thoughts, neither are your ways My ways," declares the Lord."
ISAIAH 55:8 NIV

DECLARATION 30: "GOD IS WORKING FOR MY GOOD"

I declare that:
All things are working together for my good because I love God, and I am called according to His purpose.

Everything that I am concerned about will turn around in my favor.

This is just temporary and things **WILL** get better!

SCRIPTURAL INSPIRATION:

"And we know that in all things God works for the good of those who love him, who have been called according to His purpose."

ROMANS 8:28 NIV

DECLARATION 31: "I AM WHOLE"

I declare that:
I am whole.
I am whole in my mind.
I am whole in my body.
I am whole in my soul.
I am whole in my spirit.
I am whole in Jesus Christ.
I am complete and lacking nothing.

SCRIPTURAL INSPIRATION:
"Therefore, if anyone is in Christ, he is a new creation. The old has passed away; behold, the new has come."
2 CORINTHIANS 5:17 ESV

"So you also are complete through your union with Christ, who is the head over every ruler and authority."
COLOSSIANS 2:10 NLT

"May God Himself, the God of peace, sanctify you through and through. May your whole spirit, soul and body be kept blameless at the coming of our Lord Jesus Christ."
1 THESSALONIANS 5:23 NIV

PRAYERS

PRAYERS FOR WHEN YOU'RE HURTING, FEELING LONELY, DEFEATED, SAD, OR HOPELESS

God, I'm tired of hurting and I'm tired of crying. I don't want to have these negative, self-defeating thoughts about myself and my life. I just want to trust You more, and put my hope and faith in You. Help me, Lord, to see myself the way You see me. In Jesus' name. Amen.

Fix me, Lord! Help me! I can't do this by myself anymore. I can't keep being vulnerable to men/women who don't even see my worth, don't value me or appreciate me. Lord, I know You love me, and in the right time, You will bring the right person in my life who will see my value and worth and appreciate me. Until that time, help me to rest in You and Your love, and serve and worship You. In Jesus' name. Amen.

PRAYER FOR HEALING

Heal me, Lord. Heal whatever is in me that is broken. Heal whatever is in me that is hurting. Heal the emotional wounds of my soul. Remove anything that is not like You and fill me up with more of You and the fruit of Your Spirit. In Jesus' name. Amen.

PRAYER FOR WHEN YOU ARE FEELING INSECURE

God, You are the only validation I need. You say that I am worthy of being loved. You say that I am fearfully and wonderfully made. You see a good thing in me even with all of my imperfections, and You still love me. Thank You for your consistent, unfailing love. In Jesus' name. Amen.

PRAYER FOR WHEN YOU ARE FEELING OVERWHELMED

God, I am feeling overwhelmed with life. I walk around pretending to be so strong and confident, when I am really anxious and on the verge of breaking down. God, be my strength right now. Strengthen me in the areas where I am weak. Remove all of my fears, worries, anxieties, and doubts, and replace them with more faith, hope, and trust in You. Even though it doesn't feel like it, I believe that all things are working together for my good. In Jesus' name. Amen.

PRAYER FOR IMMEDIATE HELP

Father God, right now I really do not have the words to say. God, please help me! Come quickly! I am in desperate need of You in this very moment. Give me strength right now to keep going, God, I am asking that you take over my situations that I am concerned out. Intervene on my behalf. Fight my battles right now. *Make haste, O God, to deliver me! (Psalm 70 ESV)* Please give me your peace that surpasses all understanding as I release my cares and concerns onto you. In Jesus' name, I pray. Amen.

PRAYERS WHEN YOU NEED DISCERNMENT AROUND FRIENDSHIPS AND RELATIONSHIPS

God, give me discernment to identify who no longer deserves a place in my life. Give me strength to walk away from people and situations that are purposeless and fruitless. Give me strength to keep the doors You have already closed, closed for good. Give me strength to cut off any friendships, relationships, or people whose seasons are over in my life. In Jesus' name, I pray. Amen.

Father God, give me wisdom and discernment to know the difference between a seasonal person, a frenemy, a counterfeit, or a distraction sent by the enemy. Speak to my heart and my spirit and give me discernment to know what purpose **[state the names of the person/persons]** serve in my life, and vice versa. Help me to be obedient in fulfilling whatever purpose you would like me to serve in their lives, and give me wisdom to know when my season in their lives has ended. In Jesus' name. Amen.

God, give me discernment to recognize those people who You have not called to be in journey with me at this point in my life. Please remove whomever or whatever is in my life that would hinder me from growing and maturing in You, especially those people and things that would hold me back from walking into the divine purpose You have ordained for my life. In Jesus' name, I pray. Amen.

PRAYERS WHEN YOU NEED DISCERNMENT AROUND FRIENDSHIPS AND RELATIONSHIPS *continued*

Father God, I have met a new person that I am really interested in. I ask that You give me discernment to know this person's purpose in my life, and give him/her discernment to know my purpose in being in his/her life. If you did not send this person God, please do not let me catch romantic feelings for him/her. Block it, God. However, if you did send this person into my life, bless it. In Jesus' name. Amen.

PRAYER FOR FORGIVENESS

Father God, I come to You tonight asking for forgiveness. You continue to show me when doors are closed with relationships, with (wo)men who want to date me, and You have specifically told me/revealed to me I shouldn't date them, yet I continue to put my hand back on the doorknob and open the door back up. Forgive me for being hard headed and disobedient. I hate that my flesh wants to have its own way. Please forgive me, God, for this iniquity and any other sins that I have committed in word, thought, action, or deed unknowingly and knowingly against You, myself, or anyone else. Give me strength to fight through this loneliness and to wait patiently, with hope, and in expectation on the (wo)man that You are sending with whom You have ordained for me to be in relationship. God bless my future relationship with this (wo)man and marriage to this (wo)man. In Jesus' name. Amen.

PRAYER FOR SUBMISSION TO GOD'S WILL

God, not my will, but thy will be done. I will wait on You, Lord. Have thine own way in every area of my life. Amen.

PRAYER FOR PATIENCE

God, I am feeling antsy. I am feeling as if once again I want to do something to take control of my life in the areas where I am seeking for You to change: job, relationship status, etc. Father God, I do not want to get ahead of You. God, give me patience to wait on You. You said in Your word that You would fight my battles if I only stand still. Fight my battles in these areas,

God. Help me to stand still. Give me the wisdom and discernment to know what, when, and how You want me to move in faith. Give me strength to not do anything drastic and to not do anything that is outside of Your will for me to do. Protect me from me. Stop me from hindering Your perfect will and your perfect plans in these areas of my life. Help me to put my trust in You and take my eyes off of my circumstance. In Jesus' name, I pray. Amen.

PRAYERS OF THANKSGIVING AND GRATEFULNESS

Thank you, God, for all that You are about to do for me. I decree and declare that this is my appointed time and season for breakthrough and deliverance in every area of my life. Thank You, Father God, for the release of my blessings. I decree and declare that everything is coming together for me financially, physically, mentally, spiritually, emotionally, and in my personal, romantic, and professional relationships. I thank You, God, for the manifestation of Your many blessings and promises that I've been waiting to come to fruition for so long. I ask that You continue to bless me with Your divine wisdom and knowledge so that I will understand and have clarity on how You want me to use the blessings You've given me for the building of Your kingdom. In Jesus' name, I pray. Amen.

God, You are so awesome. God, You are wonderful. God, You are everything I need You to be. God, I love You. God, I need more of You. God, I thank You for the blessings You have already given me and those that are to come. God, I thank You for Your Spirit that convicts and rebukes me, prays and intercedes for me, and leads me and guides me. Have Your way, today and every day, in my life. In Jesus' name, I pray. Amen.

God, I am so grateful for Your favor, Your grace, and Your mercy. Thank You for choosing me to be an heir of Your kingdom. Thank you for calling me friend and daughter/son. I love You so much! Amen.

Prayers of Thanksgiving and Gratefulness *continued*

Father God, thank You for another day. Thank You for life. Thank You, God, for the blessings You have bestowed on me in the past, those You are bestowing on me now in the present, and those You will bestow on me in the future. Thank You, God, in advance for making me a better person. Thank You, God, for making me more patient, compassionate to those in need, and loving to all of Your creation, even my enemies and difficult people. Thank You, God, for helping me to be quiet, talk less, and listen more. Thank You for helping me to be quick to listen and slow to anger. In Jesus' name. Amen.

Thank You, God, for increasing my faith in the area of marriage where I previously had unbelief. Thank You, God, for opening my eyes and revealing to me what I need to do and what I need to focus on in this season of my life. In Jesus' name. Amen.

God, I am simply grateful. I thank You for my life. I thank You for waking me up in my right mind, with clothes in my closet to wear, food in my refrigerator to eat, a job to go to, and a home where I rested and slept peacefully and safely. There are no words to appropriately describe my gratitude. God, You are so awesome. You are so worthy. You are so deserving of all of my praise. I bless You. I extol You. I lift Your name on high. I give You all the honor, glory, and praise. In Jesus' name. Amen!

PRAYER OF GRATEFULNESS

God, thank You for waking me up this morning. I am grateful to see another day. I praise You, God, for I am fearfully and wonderfully made. I thank You, God, for loving me in spite of my many flaws and my sinful nature. I thank You for never leaving me or forsaking me. I thank You for always being there for me and being consistent and faithful in my life. I thank You, God, for blessing me even when I don't feel as if I deserve to be blessed. I am so not worthy of even being a servant to You, but yet You call me Your child, and You call me friend. I am grateful to know that I am loved by You. In Jesus' name, I pray. Amen.

PRAYER FOR STRENGTH TO WAIT FOR GOD'S PROMISES TO BE FULFILLED

Father God, I know that Your word will not return to You void, and it will accomplish the purpose for which it was sent. Therefore, God, as You have promised me that I am to be married, help me to trust You even when there is nothing going on in my life romantically and I have no dates. I trust that You will bring the right person for me, in your due time and your due season; not a second too early, and not a second too late. Give me strength to hold out and resist temptation and strength to resist dating just any man/woman that You have not ordained for me to date. In Jesus' name. Amen.

PRAYER ABOUT CONCERNS

Thank You, Lord, for being concerned with all of the things that I'm concerned about: small things, medium things, big things. Thank You in advance for resolving all of my concerns. I know and believe that You have good plans set up for me that will bring me to a good future. In Jesus' name. Amen.

PRAYER FOR FORGIVENESS AND RELEASE OF BURDENS

Father God, remove any bitterness or unforgiveness in my heart toward anything or anybody. Help me to forgive myself for past mistakes I have made that were out of Your will. Help me to release anything that is troubling or burdening me, and give me strength to cast it all on You. In Jesus' name. Amen.

PRAYER FOR YOUR FUTURE SPOUSE

God, I pray for my husband/wife today. I pray that You would help him/her to resist the devil so that the devil will flee from pursuing him/her. Father God, give him/her the strength to not give in to temptation. Guard his/her heart, Lord. Give him/her a discerning spirit to realize and recognize what he/she needs to know about people, places, and things pertaining to him/her personally, romantically, spiritually, and professionally. In Jesus' name, I pray. Amen.

PRAYER FOR LEADING AND GUIDANCE FOR GOD'S PURPOSE FOR THE DAY

Thank You, God for waking me up with purpose. Speak to my heart, Lord, and lead me, guide me, and show me what needs to be done this day. Order my steps and guide my feet to do Your will and to complete the purpose that You have for me this day. In Jesus' name, I pray. Amen.

PRAYER OF RELEASE OF FEAR, AND DECLARATION OF INCREASE IN TRUST IN GOD

Father God, I realized today that I have a fear of never falling in love and staying in love. I have a fear that I will never get married. Thank You, Holy Spirit, for revealing these things to me. I cast down, rebuke, and bind that spirit of fear right now in the name of Jesus. God, You did not give me a spirit of fear, but of power and love and a sound mind. Today, I decree and declare that I will put my trust in You and will continue to have faith that You will bring the right person in my life. God, I decree and declare that I would trust You even when nothing is going on in my life romantically, and I don't know when my single status will change. Help me to focus on You, Your word, and walking forth in Your will and Your purpose in this season of my life. In Jesus' name, I pray. Amen.

PRAYER FOR STRENGTHENING OF FAITH AND TRUST AND ASKING FOR GOD'S PREPARATION

God I trust you in every area of my life. Strengthen my faith in the areas of my life where I have doubts, fear, anxiety, worry, and help my unbelief. Prepare me God for my blessings, and give me strength for my journey. Give me your divine wisdom and knowledge for the next levels to which you are elevating me so that I will know how to navigate and be successful on these levels. Give me insight and vision now that will prepare me for my elevation. Work on my character, my attitude, and my demeanor so that I can be fully ready for my next level of blessings. Open up doors for me that no man or woman can close. Provide me with the tools, money, and resources to do the things that You are calling me to do. In Jesus' name, I pray. Amen.

PRAYER FOR CHANGE AND TRANSFORMATION

Father God, I want to be changed and transformed. I want to be more like You in all of my ways. Help me, Lord, to be transformed by the renewal of my mind. Please forgive me, God, for my sins and iniquities. Create in me a clean heart, O God, and renew a right spirit within me. Free me for joyful obedience to Your will, Your commandments, and Your purpose for my life. Help me to walk upright and pursue holiness and righteousness all of the days of my life. In Jesus' name. Amen.

PRAYER TO BE MORE LIKE GOD

Father God, remove anything within me that is not like You and replace it with the fruit of Your spirit. Help me to be holy for You are holy. Help me to walk in love and peace. Help me to be kind, compassionate, loving, and hear and respond to the needs and cries of Your people. Help me to be obedient to do what You ask me to do. Help me to not judge and be envious of those living in the world or those of the world. Help me, Lord, to keep my mind renewed daily and be transformed in mind, body, soul, and spirit. Please forgive me for those times I have sinned knowingly or unknowingly in word, thought, action, or deed against you, myself, or anyone else. Please do not hold my sins, transgressions, or iniquities against me. Create in me a clean heart, O God, and renew a right spirit within me. Cast me not out of thy presence, O Lord, and take not thy Holy Spirit from me. Restore to me the joy of Your salvation, O God, and grant me a willing spirit to sustain me. In Jesus' name. Amen.

PRAYER REQUESTING GOD'S HELP TO REFLECT HIS LIGHT AND HIS IMAGE

Dear God, thank You for waking me up this day! Thank You, God, for allowing me to see and experience another day that I have never seen before. God, help me to do what is right by You today. Help me to obey Your word and Your will for my life. Lord, help me to be a light that reflects Your image. God, help me to be like Your Son Jesus in everything that I do or say today. In Jesus' name, I pray. Amen.

PRAYER TO BECOME BETTER AND MORE LIKE GOD

Lord God, I strive to be a better person so I can be the woman/man You want me to be and need me to be. God, I am so thankful for everything You have done and are doing in my life. I will continue to give You praise and the glory all of the days of my life. Continue to lead me and guide me in every area of my life. Make my crooked places straight and my rough places smooth. As You elevate me and take me to new levels in my life, help me to remain humble. Father God, show me and reveal to me how You want me to use my God-given gifts and talents for Your glory and for the building and uplifting of Your kingdom. Give me an obedient and willing spirit to do whatever You reveal to me and show me what needs to be done. In Jesus' name. Amen.

PRAYER OF RELEASE OF REQUESTS AND CONCERNS

God, help me to not be anxious or worried about anything, but through prayer and supplication let my requests be known unto You. These are the requests and concerns that are in my mind and on my heart this morning: *[Say your requests or concerns out loud.]* God, I thank You in advance for hearing and answering my prayers. I also thank You for supplying every one of my needs according to Your riches in glory through Christ Jesus. Thank You, God, for being Jehovah Jireh, my provider. Thank You for blessing and keeping me in every aspect of my life. In Jesus' name. Amen.

PRAYER FOR REVELATION OF AREAS WHERE MORE FAITH AND TRUST IN GOD ARE NEEDED

Father God, thank You for increasing my faith and belief in You on a daily basis. Reveal to me the areas of my life where I need to put more faith and trust in You. *[Pause for a moment and listen to God as He speaks to you.]* In these areas that You have revealed to me where I struggle in my faith and trust in You, God, help my unbelief. I cast out doubt, fear, and worry right now, and I bind and rebuke them in the name of Jesus and with the blood of Jesus. Increase my faith, hope, and trust in these areas: *[State the areas that God has revealed to you.]* In Jesus' name, I pray. Amen.

PRAYER WHEN FACING TEMPTATION

God, I come to You in need of immediate help. I am struggling in this very moment. I am feeling tempted to have sex. I am feeling tempted to text or call someone with whom I would like to be intimate. Father God, it is my desire to remain celibate while I am dating in order to please You as I know this body You have given me is Your vessel. God, You said in Your word in 1 Corinthians 10:13 NIV that *"No temptation has overtaken you except what is common to mankind. And God is faithful; he will not let you be tempted beyond what you can bear. But when you are tempted, he will also provide a way out so that you can endure it."* Therefore, God, I am asking that You shut down every sexual or lustful thought in my mind, remove these sexual feelings and lust that I am experiencing right now, and give me strength to resist doing anything sexual or intimate that I really do not wish to do. Provide a way of escape for me right now! In Jesus' mighty and powerful name, I pray. Amen.

PRAYER WHEN FEELING GUILTY AFTER FALLING INTO TEMPTATION

Father God, I am coming to You right now with a heavy heart. I have fallen into temptation and committed a sin of intimacy and/or sex with someone who is not my husband/wife. I feel guilty. I feel ashamed to even come before You right now. God, please forgive me, and please help me to forgive myself and release these feelings of shame and guilt. Jesus died for my sins so I realize that as I confess my sins to You right now, You will forgive me of my sins and my iniquities and cleanse me of all unrighteousness. I repent of committing this sin, and I ask that You remove any lingering desires to do anything remotely sexual or intimate with this person again, or with anyone else new, and give me strength to remain abstinent from this point forward until I am married. Thank You, Father God, for forgiving me and hearing my prayer. In Jesus' name, I pray. Amen.

PRAYER WHEN FEELING JEALOUS AND/OR TIRED OF WAITING

God, I come to You right now asking for and needing Your help. God, someone else I know has gotten engaged (or married), and I am in my feelings and feeling jealous right now. God, it seems like every time I turn around, I see another person getting engaged or married on my Facebook or Instagram timeline, and once again, I am left wondering when will it be my turn? God, sometimes I really get tired of waiting. I want to be married and have a family as well. I want to be happy for the people I know without feeling jealous, but in my flesh, this is what I feel from time to time. Forgive me, God, for feeling jealous and coveting someone else's blessing. I know that in Your due time, You will bless me with my husband/wife. Give me strength and patience to wait, without jealousy, but to wait the right way, with hopeful expectation and to celebrate those who are getting engaged and married. My season is coming! **It SHALL come to pass!** I will wait on You, God. Not my timing, but in Your due timing, have Your way and bring the person You have for me in my life. I thank You in advance, God, for the one that is to come. In Jesus' name. Amen.

PRAYER WHEN FEELING INSECURE AND/OR NOT GOOD ENOUGH/WORTHY OF RECEIVING LOVE

God, sometimes I think to myself, and I wonder if I am good enough, pretty (or handsome) enough, holy enough or worthy enough of receiving love and being married. I am having one of these moments right now, God. I wonder if there is something wrong with me that makes people overlook me. I feel that I am a great catch. I know that I am a work in progress who is constantly evolving and growing and becoming a better person spiritually, emotionally, mentally, and physically. But God, I just wonder why it has not happened for me yet. God, Your word reassures me in this moment. You said that I am made in your image and that I am fearfully and wonderfully made. Nothing about me is a mistake. I am uniquely designed and created in a way that pleases You. Help me to see myself as You see me, God, and help me to like myself, and to love myself more, beyond the flaws, imperfections and quirky things that I may not like about myself. I am Yours. I am a child of God. There is nothing wrong with me. I am not too much or too little of anything. I am becoming who You want me to be more and more each day, and one day, someone will appreciate all that I am now, and all that I am becoming. I thank You, God, for validating, reassuring, and loving me. In Jesus' name, I pray. Amen.

PRAYER FOR BREAKING UNGODLY SOUL TIES

Father God, I come to You today admitting that in the past, I have joined myself personally, romantically, or sexually with ungodly or demonic persons to whom I had no business being connected. I allowed these persons in my life, along with everything else that they brought with them: demonic spirits, and negative or ungodly behaviors, characteristics, and traits. In the name of Jesus, I bind, rebuke, and cut off every ungodly soul tie to these persons: *[Be still and quiet and then ask God to reveal the persons to you and then name the persons one by one.]* Father God, I ask that You sever the ties to these persons and burn the ties with Your Holy Ghost fire so that they can never, ever be reconnected to me! Close these doors to these persons for good! Give me strength to never revisit, call, email, text, or stalk them on social media, and also give me the strength to not reopen any doors to them after You cut them out of my life. Keep a hedge of protection around of me so that nothing or no one demonic or ungodly can get near me or enter into my life ever again. Cover me from the top of my head to the soles of my feet with the blood of Jesus. In Jesus' name, I pray. Amen.

SINGLE AND SET APART AFFIRMATION STATEMENT

I, **[state your name]**, rededicate my life to living for God in my single season. I am single and set apart as I am a work in progress who is constantly growing spiritually, mentally, emotionally, and physically, evolving, being purged, processed, and molded into the woman/man of God that God is shaping me to be. I submit my life and every area of my life to God and give Him permission to have His way and to do whatever He wants to do, however He wants to do it, in His perfect and divine timing. Yes, I am single. Yes, I am set apart. However, this is my portion only for this season of my life. **If it is in God's will, I shall and will be married!** In Jesus' name. Amen!

ABOUT THE AUTHOR

A native of Atlanta, Georgia, Monique C. Baisden is a single woman of God who is passionate about using her God-given gifts and talents to inspire, encourage, motivate others. Her purpose in life is to help others, and her calling is one of a servant-leader and change agent who has been called to transform and change her community and the world.

She writes to inspire. Whether she is writing prayers and declarations for single Christians, or encouraging books of inspiration for dreamers and dreamchasers, through her writing, it is her hope and prayer that people's lives are transformed, and they are inspired to pursue their dreams, walk fearlessly and authentically in their God-given purpose and calling, and be fulfilled in every area of their lives, in every season of their lives.